O9-ABI-924

Police Officer

by **Dana Meachen Rau**

Reading Consultant: Nanci R. Vargus, Ed.D.

Marshall Cavendish
Benchmark
New York

Picture Words

 car

 cars

 dog

horse

 police car

 police officer

3

A  works in town.

A drives a .

A rides a .

A  works with a .

A  stops a fast .

A fills out a
speeding ticket.

14

A  comes to help.

A shows where to go.

A  is there for you.

Words to Know

speeding ticket
    a note to pay a fine for driving
    too fast

town
    a place where people live
    and work

Find Out More

Books

Adamson, Heather. *A Day in the Life of a Police Officer*. Mankato, MN: Capstone Press, 2006.

Gordon, Sharon. *What's Inside a Police Car?* Tarrytown, NY: Marshall Cavendish, 2004.

Murphy, Patricia J. *The Police Station*. Mankato, MN: Pebble Plus, 2004.

Owen, Ann. *Keeping You Safe: A Book about Police Officers*. Minneapolis, MN: Picture Window Books, 2006.

Videos

Amazing Heroes: Spend a Day with Police Officers. First Look Pictures, 2003.

Web Sites

Department of Justice: Justice for Kids and Youth
http://www.usdoj.gov/kidspage

National Crime Prevention Council: McGruff the Crime Dog
http://www.mcgruff.org

About the Author

Dana Meachen Rau is an author, editor, and illustrator. A graduate of Trinity College in Hartford, Connecticut, she has written more than two hundred books for children, including nonfiction, biographies, early readers, and historical fiction. She lives with her family in Burlington, Connecticut.

About the Reading Consultant

Nanci R. Vargus, Ed.D., wants all children to enjoy reading. She used to teach first grade. Now she works at the University of Indianapolis. Nanci helps young people become teachers.

Marshall Cavendish Benchmark
99 White Plains Road
Tarrytown, NY 10591-9001
www.marshallcavendish.us

All Internet addresses were correct at the time of printing.

Library of Congress Cataloging-in-Publication Data

Rau, Dana Meachen, 1971–
Police officer / by Dana Meachen Rau.
    p. cm. – (Benchmark rebus)
Summary: "Easy to read text with rebuses explores the job duties of a police officer"—Provided by publisher.
Includes bibliographical references.
ISBN 978-0-7614-2618-9
1. Police—Juvenile literature. I. Title. II. Series.
HV7922.R38 2007
363.2'3—dc22
2006037704

Editor: Christine Florie
Publisher: Michelle Bisson
Art Director: Anahid Hamparian
Series Designer: Virginia Pope

Photo research by Connie Gardner

Rebus images provided courtesy of *Dorling Kindersley*.

Cover photo by Benn Mitchell/Getty

The photographs in this book are used with permission and through the courtesy of:
PhotoEdit: p. 5 Robert Brenner; p. 11 Rudi Von Briel; *Alamy*: p. 7 Rieger Bertrand/Hemispheres Images; p. 13 D. Hurst;
p. 17 Richard Levine; *Corbis*: p. 9 Tony Aruzza; p. 21 Bernd Oberman; *The Image Works*: p. 15 Bangor Daily News;
p. 19 Chet Cordon.

Printed in Malaysia
1 3 5 6 4 2